BEGIN WITH PRAYER

BEGIN WITH PRAYER

Openings for Church Group Meetings

Kenneth W. Rogahn

Publishing House
St. Louis

BV
250
R64
1985

Copyright © 1985 by Concordia Publishing House
3558 South Jefferson Ave., St. Louis, MO 63118
Manufactured in the United States of America

Rogahn, Kenneth, 1933-
        Begin with prayer.

        Rev. ed. of: Open the meeting with prayer / Harry N. Hux-
hold. 1973.
        1. Prayers. I. Huxhold, Harry N. Open the meeting with
prayer. II. Title.
BV250.R64 1985   264'.13   84-22961
ISBN 0-570-03962-2

---

1 2 3 4 5 6 7 8 9 10 MAL 94 93 92 91 90 89 88 87 86 85

CONTENTS

PREFACE

For those occasions when lay leaders are asked to conduct opening and closing devotions for church group meetings, *Begin with Prayer* provides a variety of resources. Replacing *Open the Meeting with Prayer*, this new book adjusts to present-day circumstances in the church and offers, in addition to a selection of prayers for each organization or group, appropriate Scripture readings, and optional hymns.

Group leaders may use the prayers and outlines for devotions as they appear in the book or adapt them to fit local situations and time schedules. Preferably, adequate time should be set aside for preparation and for the exercise of group devotions, though this book should provide at least the essential elements of a meaningful worship service.

May the guidance and blessing of the Triune God accompany the use of these resources to the glory and service of Christ, the Head of the church.

—THE PUBLISHER

AN ORDER FOR OPENING A MEETING

Leader: In the name of the Father and of the Son and of the Holy Spirit.

All: AMEN.

Scripture reading and hymn appropriate to the meeting may be read or sung. Suggestions are listed in each category of prayers in this book.

Prayer for the meeting (see appropriate page in this book)

All: AMEN.

AN ORDER FOR CLOSING A MEETING

Leader: Let us all speak the Apostles' Creed.

All: I BELIEVE IN GOD THE FATHER ALMIGHTY, etc.

Leader: We pray together the prayer our Lord taught.

All: OUR FATHER, WHO ART IN HEAVEN . . . , etc.

Leader: May the grace of the Lord Jesus Christ

and the love of God our Father and the fellowship of His Holy Spirit be with us all.

All: AMEN.

ALTAR GUILD OR COMMITTEE

Read: Ps. 24 or 26; Luke 2:36-38; 2 Chronicles 6:18-21
Sing: Here, O my Lord, I see You face to face or, O day of rest and gladness

Heavenly Father, angels and archangels and all the company of heaven join with Your saints on earth and in heaven to give You thanks and praise. We offer our lives to You, and give You service in Your house, because You have called us to be Your people. Guide our efforts to prepare the holy articles in this place of worship, so that they may bring others closer to You. Make us diligent and joyful in all that we do. Remind us that we serve You as we serve Your people. We give ourselves to these holy and humble tasks, so that Your presence may be known and felt by those who gather here to worship You. We pray for those who will come together for worship in Your church, those who will lead and all who follow. Give us a glad satisfaction in doing our work well, through Jesus Christ our Lord. **Amen.**

L ord Jesus Christ, like the women who minis-
tered to You in Your days on earth in the flesh,
we gladly give our time and effort to serve You.
We believe that You are present with Your people
through Word and Sacrament, and we prepare
Your way as we care for the place where You
meet with all who have come to You. Guide and
encourage us for our tasks and duties. Clear our
minds from distractions and keep us from carelessness. We come here to work with reverence
and hope, so that You may be better seen and
known in all Your majesty and kindness. Accept
the service of your hands, for we offer ourselves
in joyful response to Your call. And You are
Christ, the Lord. **Amen.**

O Holy Spirit, in You we worship the Father
and by You we know that Jesus is the true
and living Way. Renew our spirits so that we may
obediently carry out the responsibilities here entrusted to us. Transform us by our contact with
the holy things of God and of His church, for You
give life and power when and where it pleases
You. As we near the altar, recall to our minds
Christ's sacrifice for us. In the light of the candles,
show us the light that came into the darkness of
the world. Through the water and bread and wine
of the holy sacraments, which convert and enlighten God's people, give us joy and peace. By
the fellowship into which You have called us, we

are privileged to make ready the way of Christ. Give us a spirit of care and concern for all who will use these sacred items, so that we may carefully and prayerfully do our part. Hear and answer us, as we pray in Jesus' name. **Amen.**

God, our Father in heaven, we are both pleased and awed that You choose to come among us. Be present in grace and power during the time that we give to these special duties.

God the Father's only Son, we adore Your holy name and bless You for Your life and death and resurrection. Let us experience these saving events by faith and help others to share them through the work we do.

God the Holy Spirit, You move among us like the wind and kindle in our hearts the fire of Your holy love. Inspire us to give our witness by serving those whom You gather and enlighten and sanctify.

Holy Trinity, God for us and in us, use our hands, our talents, our skills, our minds, our hearts, our faith to please You and edify others. **Amen.**

BIBLE CLASS

Read: Ps. 19:7-14 or Psalm 119 (any section); John 1:1-13; 2 Tim. 3:14-16

Sing: God's Word is our great heritage or, O Word of God incarnate

Heavenly Father, Your direction and inspiration of the writers of past ages preserved Your Word for us. We thank You for the opportunity to read and grow by Your Word to mankind. Bless us as we gather together. We study and share as we search the Scriptures with one another. Grant that they may testify to us of Jesus Christ, so that we may know Him by the message of the apostles and prophets as the chief Cornerstone. Make us ready to hear and to speak, to help one another and to share the testimony which gives glory to You. Give us sharpness of mind and thought. Make us grow in wisdom and in Your favor. Answer our prayer and speak to us, for Christ's sake. **Amen.**

Jesus, Word of God incarnate, You are the Revealer of the Father, Promise-Keeper for the Father. We praise You for continuing to teach Your people who read the Bible and open their minds and lives to You. Make us receptive. Let Your Word produce fruit in our lives. Keep us from only hearing Your Word and not doing it.

Direct us so that we may bring forth things old and new from the pages of Holy Scripture. We confess that You cannot be contained even in all the books written in the world, for You are the Lord. But we are truly grateful that we can meet You here and be richer in grace as we listen to Your voice. Without You we would not know the truth about ourselves or the true God. Intercede for us with the Father so that He will send His Spirit to help us. By our own understanding or effort we cannot believe in You, so help us, our Savior. **Amen.**

Spirit of God, You spoke by the prophets. You inspired the apostles. You have always enlightened and comforted God's people. Without You we cannot hear our Lord's voice or come to Him. Forgive us for thinking that our learning or our wisdom can give understanding of the deep things of God. You are the Lord of life and power. Teach us in the ways we should go. Inspire us to be the people of God in the world today. Our thoughts and words can never fully express our need. Intercede for us with sighs and pleadings and bring the Father's blessing to us. It is good that our Lord sent You as Comforter and Counselor, to make real for us what has been written as a guide for our lives. Teach us, O Lord, for the sake of Jesus Christ, in whose name we pray. **Amen.**

Heavenly Father, You revealed Yourself to us and to our world. The testimony of Your special witnesses has been preserved for us through all ages. Give us a new and helpful revelation of Yourself in this present time.

Helping Son, You came into this world to reveal the Father's truth and grace. We worship You as our Mediator and Friend. Teach us as You taught Your disciples in those days.

Holy Spirit, You alone can give meaning to the texts and words that we study. Help us truly understand and rightly believe the Word of God. Show us that more remains to be seen and experienced by all of us here.

Loving and gracious God, we will never know all that You are and do. Guarantee that as we search the Scriptures, we may find eternal life by the message that testifies to Your Word for us, even Jesus Christ, our Lord. **Amen.**

BOARD OF DIRECTORS OR CHURCH COUNCIL

Read: Ps. 133; Acts 6:1-6; 2 Cor. 5:6-10
Sing: Built on the Rock, the church shall stand
or, O Holy Spirit, enter in

Almighty God, You are the Ruler of nations and Director of the universe. You control all the events of life. In Your goodness You will use Your might for the well-being and salvation of people. And so we give You thanks for directing our lives until we have found rest in You. We meet today to serve You and to conduct the affairs of this congregation. Give us knowledge and strength to do Your will, with a proper balance of eternal values and present needs. Give us concern for all the people of this church and awareness of those who are outside our fellowship. Let us all properly carry out the responsibilities of our offices, decently and in order. Grant us boldness to act in Your name and caution to consider the feelings of other people. Bless what we do here, for Jesus' sake. **Amen.**

Lord Jesus Christ, during Your ministry on earth You called disciples to follow You. You have experienced the temptations and dangers of earthly leadership. You know the disappointments and fears that trouble those who seek to serve the Father. By Your perfect life and death You have earned for us the right to be heard and helped. We pray for what we need at this meeting in order to carry out the Father's will. Share the power of Your resurrection with us, so that in newness of life we may serve others. Give us perspective and awareness of what You desire for us to do. Keep us from self-centeredness and pettiness in our dealings with our fellow members. Grant us that we are honest and good in our decisions. Guide Your church in this place, through us and for Your name's sake. **Amen.**

L ord, Holy Spirit, Your sacred inspiration guided and protected God's people in every age. We seek Your wisdom now: show us what pleases the Father. We ask that Your direction in our discussions allows the business of this congregation to proceed in a good manner. We who have been entrusted with roles of leadership, often do not know what to say or do. Convince us that by Your help we can do well. We want to share ideas and plans with each other. We want to further Your causes and benefit many people. Keep us courteous and kind to one another. Direct our attention to the work at hand. Let neither pride or laziness control our meeting. Give us strength to resist all temptations to dominate or to desert, to control or coerce, to forget or to fail. We pray through Christ, our Lord. **Amen.**

F ather, You have all wisdom. Every good and perfect gift comes from You. Look with pity and favor upon us who are gathered here for this meeting.

Lord Jesus, You gave Your life for the salvation of the world. Be present with us as we seek to continue your saving work in our world today.

God the Spirit, You regenerated us when we were dead in trespasses and sins. Refresh us by Your life-saving power today, so we use wisely the life You have given us.

O God, bless us. Keep us. Shine upon us. Be gracious to us. Look upon us with favor. Grant us Your peace. **Amen.**

BOARD OF TRUSTEES

Read: Ps. 65; Titus 2:11-14; Acts 4:32-35
Sing: I love Your kingdom, Lord or, Our God, our help in ages past

O Lord, You cannot be restricted to one place. All heaven and earth cannot contain You. And yet You choose special places where You come to be with Your people and to reveal Yourself. We thank You for the opportunity we have to provide for the facilities and property of this congregation. We thank You for the gifts You have given us to use in this great task. Grant us a proper relation to the things of this world and the world to come. Make us good stewards of the blessings which You give us and which we presume to call ours. Let us neither neglect our responsibility nor imagine that You need our help to preserve this church. We are glad to serve You and we ask You to lead us to serve You well, through Jesus Christ, our Lord. **Amen.**

Lord, our God, accept our efforts to serve You by the wise use of the earthly resources at our command. Do not let us become so busy with what is in our hands that we ignore what is in our hearts. We are custodians of tangible and real property. Keep our minds aware of the one thing needful to our well-being and to the life of Your church here. Show us how those things which are unseen become real in the physical realities of our existence. Help us to be businesslike in our transactions and yet to be about our Father's business. Let us care for our congregation's assets wisely. Keep us innocent as doves. In the name and Spirit of Jesus we pray. **Amen.**

BOARD
OF EDUCATION

Read: Ps. 112; Mark 8:34-38; 2 Cor. 13:5-9
Sing: Dearest Jesus, at Your Word or, On my
heart imprint Your image

Lord God, teach us what is Your will, so that we can help others to teach and learn. The ignorance and rejection of Your teaching in our world today leads us to confess that we too do not know all that You want to teach us. So we open ourselves to instruction. Enlighten our minds and hearts by Your holy Word. Let the words of our mouths and the meditations of our hearts be acceptable to You. Give us Your teachings, Your instruction, Your precepts, Your will, Your laws, Your ways, Your statutes, Your ordinances, Your testimonies, Your promises, Your truths, Your judgments, Your Word, and the insight to know how they testify to Jesus. Grant that we share knowledge in the plans and decisions that we make in this meeting. For Jesus' sake. **Amen.**

Divine Teacher, You have done all that is needed so that we may inherit eternal life. Teach us how to share that saving knowledge with others. Help us to train our children in Your ways. It is good to be here and to share eternal truths with one another. We have not yet attained nor are we already perfect. We follow You and desire with others to learn all that You have commanded us. Watch over all the schools and classes of Your church and especially of this congregation. Make teachers and students friends and helpers of one another, instead of enemies and competitors. Fill our lips with gracious words. Fill all the earth with the knowledge of the Lord. Let each his lesson learn with care, so all Your household well may fare. In Your name we ask it. **Amen.**

Spirit of the living God, recreate us. Make us dead to sin and alive to righteousness, ready for the duties in the area of education here in our congregation. Combine earthly and heavenly knowledge in all the educational agencies of our church, so that everyone benefits now and eternally. Restrain those who search for accomplishment and knowledge but turn away from You. Forgive us when we prefer our own ideas to Yours. You alone can search the deep things of God and teach our spirits those spiritual truths and spiritual words that will make us bearers of salvation to others. Call us to learn from You, and make our learning a pleasant and pleasing task. Open our eyes to see the wonderful things God has prepared for those who love him. Give us a share in them, through Jesus Christ. **Amen.**

Loving God, You ordained and established all that is and has been and will be. Give us openness to You and to what You reveal to us. Then we will benefit from Your grace.

Obedient Son, grant that we may also learn from what we suffer and grow by what we are taught. Conform us to Your image.

Powerful Spirit, draw us to the Father and Son. Send us forward in divine love to convey rich blessings to others.

God, Father, Son, and Holy Spirit: accept our thanks for Your rich grace to us. Open us to Your direction. Offer life and salvation to all through us. Make us impatient with those who are indolent. Keep us tolerant with those who are trying. **Amen.**

BUILDING COMMITTEE

Read: Ps. 48 or 84 or 127; 1 Cor. 3:10-17
Sing: Glorious things of You are spoken or, Open
now Your gates of beauty

O Lord, we prepare to build on Your behalf. We know that our labor will not be good if we do it without You. So we begin in Your name, confessing our limitations and seeking Your help. We have so many factors to consider in plans and designs, materials and form, workers and super- visors, weather and time, relationships and co- operation. And all of them must come together properly before our project may be completed. We offer You our good intentions and our best efforts. Direct them and correct them, so our hopes become reality. Watch over our building in each step along the way to its completion. By our success here prepare us for our participation in Your eternal day, when You shall raise us up to everlasting life, through Jesus Christ, our Lord. **Amen.**

Heavenly Father, powers that destroy are strong in this world. We need to be encour- aged by Your promise to build up what others cannot tear down. Your Son has promised that even death and hell cannot prevail against His church. We are bold to begin our work in His name. Help us to use our knowledge and the abilities of others to do the job that is before us. Guide us along the way. Do not let delays and problems discourage us or delay us. Keep us from the improper pride that boasts of what we have built here. Make us aware that we are Your instruments for raising up lasting signs of Your presence and activity in the world. Show us how to build up the faith of others as we construct this edifice, for we pray to You in Jesus' name. **Amen.**

CHOIR

Read: Ps. 95:1-7 or 98 or 147; Matt. 21:14-16; Eph. 5:15-20

Sing: Come, let us join our cheerful songs or, Oh, that I had a thousand voices

Almighty God, You are worthy of praise and adoration. Direct us as we practice and prepare to lead others to You in worship. Give us psalms and hymns and spiritual songs to sing, to express our gladness and gratitude for all Your love to us. Like the perfect harmony of the universe You created, blend our voices and our wills together into one. Let each of us contribute and offer what is unique so that the total presentation may please You and all who hear us. Help our leader to be firm and helpful in directing us, so we may follow him/her and produce one harmonious sound. Let us all with gladsome voice praise You, the God of heaven and earth. We ask it in Jesus' name. **Amen.**

Lord Jesus, even the stones would praise You if human voices were silent. But we will speak and sing to You and tell others about You and Your marvelous love for us, by our music and presence in the gathering of worshipers. Combine our minds and our spirits in prayer and praise that others can understand and appreciate. We thank You for the ability to be singers and leaders in this choir. Convince us that we have a gift to offer You in our singing. Keep us mindful that You have given us the ability that we now employ in Your service. Hear the hosanna and hallelujah we sing, for they express our faith and hope in You, our Lord and Savior and King. **Amen.**

Spirit of God, Breath of life, Wind in the world, without You we would not be living beings, nor could we raise the sounds and tones of our doxology. How marvelously You inspire our mortal bodies with Your power and presence. How powerfully You use our frames to sound words and notes that bring life to the world. How beautifully You tune us so we may sing glad songs. Keep us from spoiling the symphony that You are producing through us, by our sour notes or prideful individuality. Make us willing to concentrate on music that is plain and familiar and music that is intricate and new. You fill the world and at the beginning enlivened Adam to be a living creature. Fill us too with Your mysterious life, and let others know You in us, through Jesus Christ our Lord. **Amen.**

Father in heaven, we sing to You because You have spoken to us. You put on our lips a new song of the marvelous things You have done to save us. Accompany and support us in the sounds we make and the songs we sing.

Lord Jesus, You are God's Word made flesh for us. Use our human flesh also to bring grace and truth to others. Our skills and abilities are at Your disposal, so that we may minister to others.

Holy Spirit, give us breath to praise the Lord and wills to be obedient to Him. Give us unity and the bond of peace to produce a harmony of music and people.

God, our God, we Your children on earth praise You and give all glory to You by our music and lives. Fill us with melody and use us according to Your will. **Amen.**

CONGREGATIONAL MEETING

Read: Ps. 40; Luke 17:7-10; 1 Cor. 12:4-13
Sing: Christ, whose glory fills the skies or, The church's one foundation

God our Father, we gather in Your name to carry out the work of Your church and to conduct the business of this congregation. Help us to proceed with all matters in proper order, to seek Your kingdom and righteousness and then to add all the other things that make up our lives. We recognize how easily and how quickly our priorities delay what is of special interest to You because we occupy our time with what we think is most important. Give us a vision of all Your plan and of our part in Your saving work. Give wisdom and discretion to our leader, to conduct our business meeting wisely. Grant us the patience to hear reports and to consider decisions with adequate attention. Keep us moving forward when we are tempted to delay. Into Your hands we commend ourselves and our actions, for the sake of Christ our Lord. **Amen.**

Lord Jesus, You have called us to follow You. In the same way that You came into this world to serve and to give Your life as a ransom, we want to be servants and ministers too. Help us to measure our resources and our opportunities, and to match them to one another. May every individual give thought to his/her place in the work that You have set before us. May we all consider even the smallest and least significant person affected by our decisions. We confess that much has been left undone. We know that even when we do all, we are still unprofitable servants. But You have done all things well. You have done everything to gain us the Father's favor. You will do Your will through us. So use us now, Christ, our Lord. **Amen.**

Holy Spirit, show us what seems good to You, as we gather to carry out the plans and work of our congregation. Create in us clean hearts. Renew right spirits within us. Help us to know what You want us to do. Make us willing to do it. Keep in our minds the memory of those who have gone before us and established Your work in this place. Grant us the vision to consider those who will come after us and will inherit our accomplishments and our mistakes. Free us from the need to be right for our own sake, to defend our own reputation from all criticism, to justify our existence by suggesting that we always know what is best. Use every part of Your church. Shape us to fit together and to work together. Then shall You receive the praise, with the Father and the Son, forever and ever. **Amen.**

We know Your power, Father in heaven, and we know Your love. We speak to You as dear children to their dear father.

We confess Your grace, Jesus, and we acknowledge You as Lord. We ask You to correct us and return us to the path You walked.

We declare Your influence, gracious Spirit, and we recognize Your mystery. We are ready to open ourselves to new possibilities.

Be close to us, our God. Continue what is good and begin what is helpful.

Be firm with us, our God. Occupy our time and our meeting with interests that are Yours.

Be gracious for us, our God. Forgive us so we forgive one another as brothers (and sisters) in Christ.

We pray in the name of Jesus. **Amen.**

A Litany

(The leader will announce the responses in advance)

God our Father,
God the Son,
God the Holy Spirit:
 HAVE MERCY ON US
For the time to discuss and report,
For the opportunity to vote and decide,
For the setting out of plans and hopes:
 WE THANK YOU, LORD
For guidance to pastors and teachers,
For knowledge of Your will and ways,
For sensitivity to people's needs and fears:
 WE THANK YOU, LORD

For direction in our church's mission,
For protection from disunity in spirit,
For confession of faith as we serve:
    WE THANK YOU, LORD
We pray for knowledge and strength. Make us
       ready to obey.
We pray for forgiveness and love. Let us give and
       receive.
We pray for peace and joy. Share Your gifts with
       us.
    Lord, in Your mercy:
    HEAR OUR PRAYER

Equip us with all the skills and abilities that we need in order to know and to carry out the plans You have for our congregation, through Christ, our Lord. **Amen.**

Lord, our God, we are here because we want to serve You and do Your will. What do You want us to do? We set aside our own needs and problems for a time to work together. How can we become more aware of others? We have many questions about what to do in our congregation and community. Where do You want us to go? We are Christians together and yet we have much that separates us from one another. Who can inspire us to fully participate in the ministry we have? We can go in many different directions or improve our present ways. When should we change and when should we continue? We are challenged by the size of the needs we face and comforted by Your promises to help. Why is it so confusing to make decisions?

Answer our questions, our Father. Help us to answer them for others, through Jesus Christ. **Amen.**

 ELDERS

Read: Ps. 50; Matt. 18:15-20; John 14:12-17; 1 Thess. 5:14-22

Sing: Jesus sinners will receive or, Praise to the Lord, the Almighty

God, our Father, we come before You for this hour of discussion and decision. Give us wisdom and understanding for the work that has been given to us. Call to our mind the words You have spoken and Your servants have written. Let them show us the course we need to follow. In our duties be a very present help. Accompany, encourage, and guide us as we comfort the sick, strengthen the weak, and recall the straying. You know how much and in what ways we need Your help. We also are aware of our shortcomings and inadequacies. You know that we act in Your name only because You have designated us leaders in Your church. Give us the mind of Christ in our ministry to one another and to all people. Help us to follow Jesus and not our own preferences.

We ask it in His name. **Amen.**

Lord Jesus Christ, we mourn for those separated from You, as You wept over Jerusalem. We declare the counsel of God to those in error, as You confronted the false teachers of Israel. We nurture the weak and young, as You took the children in Your arms and blessed them. We pray that our service may have the same effect and power as Yours did. May others have richer and better lives because we are present with them, as You were. We praise Your Father for sending You into this world and granting the power to forgive sins. When we are called upon to forgive, make us kind and willing. When we must discipline, make us strong and understanding. At all times make it clear to others that we come in Your name and speak for You, our Savior. You alone make our prayers acceptable to the Father. **Amen.**

God, You are the Spirit that gives life. You gave help to Moses and to his assistants. You direct all pastors and teachers who share the gospel with us. You showered the church on Pentecost with a life-giving fountain. You still nourish this congregation today. Now we ask You to come upon us. Help us, direct us, use us. Increase faith, hope, and love among the members of this congregation. Unite us with our pastor and all who have special responsibility for the spiritual well-being of Christians. We pray for the growth and life of those committed to our care. We pray especially for those who are sick or troubled or in any distress of body, soul, or spirit. Give us a sensitivity to the needs of others and to Your presence in them and us. For Jesus' sake. **Amen.**

God, You are the Creator, Redeemer, and Sanctifier. We meet You in Word and Sacrament, as You come to us with grace and blessing. We thank You for calling us into Your kingdom. We thank You for allowing us to be members of this congregation. We thank You for appointing us as special workers with the saints in this church body. We need Your power, to work effectively and to overcome the forces of evil that frustrate Your saving intentions. We seek Your grace, to care for people as You do and to endure hostility and misunderstanding in our efforts to help. We ask that Your holiness fill our lives. Overcome in us the temptation to adopt the ways of the world for the work of Your kingdom in order to enjoy some success. You justify us by Your grace; now sanctify us also according to Your great mercy, in Christ, our Lord. **Amen.**

EVANGELISM COMMITTEE

Read: Ps. 32; Matt. 28:16-20; John 12:44-50
Sing: "Come, follow Me," said Christ, the Lord
or, Go, tell it on the mountain

God, our Father, we thank You for revealing Your Son Jesus Christ to us and for giving us eternal life in him. We admit that our flesh and blood outlook could never have given us true knowledge of the mystery of salvation. We still need Your help to free us from human notions and restrictions. Send us to others and make us ready to share the good news of Christ with many. As we plan and prepare, when we telephone or visit, in the face of opposition or rejection, whenever we are Your representatives, we cannot succeed unless You are with us. Convince us of the truth of the Gospel and the need of all people for Your love in Jesus Christ. Let us gladly and willingly bear witness to Him who carries our requests now. **Amen.**

O Jesus, the kingdom and the power and the glory are Yours forever and ever. We recall and celebrate Your mercy, for You came to this world to call sinners to repentance. We rejoice that You have called us and that through us You will invite others. We recall and celebrate Your suffering and dying to redeem us and all people.

We believe that You died for us. We recall and celebrate Your conquest of death and Your exaltation to the right hand of the Father. We call upon You to be present with us now. Accompany us in our visits and invitations to others. We recall and celebrate Your loving reception of others and how You offered paradise to all. We ask You to guide our speaking, our hearing, our responding, and our praying for others. You helped those who called us on Your behalf. Now help us, so that many more may be saved. **Amen.**

Spirit of the living God, be a fountain of living water to those who are thirsty. Grant strength to dry bones. Give tongues of testimony to the fearful. You anointed Jesus to preach good news to the poor, to proclaim release to the captives and recovering of sight to the blind, to set at liberty those who are oppressed, and to proclaim the acceptable year of the Lord. And He fufilled the Scriptures. Now fill us as well. We want to share in the continuing ministry of our Lord in the present. Let the names on our list be real people to us. Let the outline of our testimony be a framework for our faith. Let the visits we make bring Jesus into other people's homes and lives. Use what is good in us and overcome what is bad. Let others see Jesus present for them in us. In Jesus we ask. **Amen.**

FINANCE COMMITTEE

Read: Ps. 115; Matt. 22:15-22; Luke 12:13-21;
1 Tim. 6:6-10
Sing: May we Your precepts, Lord, fulfill or,
Sing to the Lord of harvest

Heavenly Father, all the treasures of the
world belong to You. You are the Giver of
all things. In our world, where money is power
and talks in commanding tones, sometimes we do
not even hear Your voice. But You are pleased
by the offerings Your people bring to You. We
are Your servants in the processing of contribu-
tions. Give us a balanced respect for cash and
finances. Keep us aware of the many evils that
are rooted in the love of money. Remind us how
it is more blessed to give than to receive. Let this
special ministry of ours be carried out with effi-
ciency and wisdom. Let the counting and record-
ing procedures promote good stewardship by us
and by all who share their resources with others.
Keep us from unknowing judgments about what
others give or do not give. Protect us from vio-
lating confidentiality about money matters. Let
our work prove that we can do all things to Your
glory, through Christ our Lord. **Amen.**

Jesus, our priceless Treasure, You were sold for
30 pieces of silver by the one who kept the

money for the disciples. We need Your help to resist the temptation that kept Judas from remaining faithful to You. Help us to do that. Those who followed You on earth gave freely of their possessions for Your support. By Your grace we gladly sacrifice for You, as we expect others to do. Help us to do that. Your apostle Paul encouraged systematic and planned giving for the needs of Your people. Strengthen us to pledge and to perform, and to count it a blessing to give rather than to receive. Help us to do that. We have sometimes endured remarks about those thieves in the temple whom You cast out as moneychangers. Grant that we serve You in purity with these financial duties. Keep us free of accusations of callousness toward others. Help us, Christ our Lord. **Amen.**

O Holy Spirit, all things are sanctified by the Word of God and prayer. We pray that You will sanctify our work and gathering. Grant that money, which could be unrighteous mammon, may be transformed into eternal investments of what has been entrusted to us. We want to render to God the things that are God's. We give obedience and trust to our Father and our Lord by the symbols of cash and coin. Show us how valuable our work can be, different from the counters of coins and recorders of receipts in the secular world. Make us good stewards and workers in Your kingdom. Praise us as shrewd servants with a knowledge of how money is to be wisely handled. Cleanse us from all unrighteousness, so that our hands when raised in prayer may be holy and we may be free of wrath and doubting. In the name of Jesus we pray. **Amen.**

KINGDOM WORKERS

Read: Ps. 46; Matt. 7:21-27; 1 Cor. 9:19-23
Sing: God loved the world so that He gave or, Hark, the voice of Jesus calling

Heavenly Father, we seek first Your kingdom and its righteousness. We believe that all other things will be added to us. You have given us all things in Christ. Give us now an awareness of our opportunities and a readiness to serve You. Let us hear the voice of Your Son calling us to be with Him. Let others hear His call through us. Answer our prayers. Supply what we need. Remove what is false. Equip us to be Your representatives and ambassadors. Grant us boldness to speak in Your name and to act without hesitation or apology. Make us kind and compassionate, loving and true. By Your grace and our efforts bring others to Your kingdom. In Christ, the King, we pray. **Amen.**

O God our Savior and King, we confess that we are weary. We can so easily be turned

aside from helping others. We admit our failure
to employ the gifts that You have given us for the
welfare and salvation of others. We make no claim
to Your continued favor except the intercession
of Your Son, Jesus Christ. He is the proclaimer
and bearer of Your almighty rule. To Him every
knee must bow. Every tongue must confess Him
as Lord. He was obedient to death, even death
on a cross. By His glorious resurrection and the
outpouring of His Spirit, we are ready to be Your
people and to share eternal life with others. Build
us up and join us together. May our lives and
efforts avail for Your cause and the salvation of
men and women around us. In Jesus' name.
Amen.

LADIES AID OR GUILD

Read: Ps. 123; Mark 12:41-44; Acts 9:36-42;
1 John 4:7-11

Sing: In You is gladness or, What a Friend we
have in Jesus

O Lord, how can we add to the good work of
all the women of faith that have preceded
us? We are grateful for those saints in Your
church and in this congregation who have so long
and so well carried on the work which Your Son

has given to all believers. Expand our view and point us to new horizons. Move us forward gladly into those projects and areas where we can do some good for others. We offer our special abilities and gifts to You in heartfelt devotion. Set them to the tasks which are before Your people today. We thank You that we may live in these times and go forward in Your name and grace to overcome evil and to set things right. Use us as You have used others. Finally give us the reward that You have promised, through Jesus Christ. **Amen.**

L ord Jesus, Savior and Friend, we are so privileged to be among those who can follow You and render You service. We believe that You continue to carry out Your saving will today. All that we have, we gladly give. Whenever we can serve, we are ready. Wherever You want us to go, we will go. We cannot all be as significant as Your servants Miriam and Hannah and Mary and Lydia, but our hearts are open to Your direction too. We are like the others whose names may never be remembered by people but are well known to You. So hear us and help us, as we set about the jobs that are waiting to be done. In all we do, grant that we remain close to You and please You too. We praise You and adore You, in word and deed, Christ, the Lord. **Amen.**

S pirit of God, Your powerful overshadowing of the Virgin Mary conceived our Lord Jesus

Christ. In the mystery of the Word made flesh, You allowed Mary to bear the Son of God and to raise Him as her own Child. We cannot comprehend this great miracle, nor can we express our gratitude for granting such great privilege to one of us. Since You have used her and others as instruments of Your mercy, so give us also the privilege of having bodies and souls as Your temples. Dwell within us. Let Jesus live in us and bless others through us. In our meeting and in the lives of each member of our group, move as You will. Remind us of all that Jesus said. Give us words and actions that witness to Him. We ask it in His name. **Amen.**

We begin our meeting in the name of the Father, who has made us heirs in His family, and of the Son, who is our Lord and our Brother by faith, and of the Holy Spirit, whose life-giving power has been seen in children born into this world and born again into God's kingdom. We gather in the name of our God, to acknowledge our sins and to share our faith. Renewed by You, almighty God, we shall see and think and act as You inspire and direct us. Sanctify our plans. Correct our errors. Guide our actions. Give us a proper sense of accomplishment for the work we are doing to serve You and Your people. We thank You for the guarantee that Your Word will accomplish whatever You want done. Make us ready to bear Your Word in voice and will, for the sake of Christ, our Lord. **Amen.**

A Litany

*(The leader will announce
the responses in advance)*

Father, in whom we live and move,
Son, by whom the world was redeemed,
Spirit, through whom we are made holy:
     HAVE MERCY ON US.
For freedom from jealousy and rivalry,
For deliverance from confusion and uncertainty,
For escape from disinterest and laziness:
     WE THANK YOU, LORD.
For help in times of rejection and failure,
For support when friends mistreat us,
For sharing of accomplishment and joy:
     WE THANK YOU, LORD.
For endurance through the drudgery of service,
For understanding of those who hurt us,
For obedience to Your good and holy will:
     WE THANK YOU, LORD.
We pray for us who are present,
     that we may be one in spirit and action.
We pray for members who are absent,
     that they may be safe and protected.
We pray for those yet to join us,
     that they may be welcomed by all.
     Lord, in Your mercy:
     HEAR OUR PRAYER.

Share Yourself with us, O Lord, so that we
may offer ourselves to one another in love and
receive one another as sisters in the faith, to Your
pleasure in Christ, our Lord. **Amen.**

MARRIED COUPLES CLUB

Read: Ps.45 or 128; Luke 20:34-39; Eph. 5:21-33
Sing: Lord Jesus Christ, be present now or, O sons and daughters of the King

Heavenly Father, from You every family in heaven and on earth is named. And You have put Your name upon us. We ask You to direct our thoughts and our activities, so that each couple here may know themselves and You in love. Let the great love with which You have loved us in Jesus Christ, bind our hearts together and raise them into Your presence. Let Your good Spirit fill our spirits with gladness and peace. Keep us from thoughts and actions that would disgrace our relationship as husband and wife. Keep us true to one another as You are true to us. Make us good for one another as You are good for us. We thank You for the opportunity to gather in Your name with other husbands and wives who are Your people, through Jesus Christ our Lord. **Amen.**

Lord Jesus, You came to the wedding at Cana to bless that married couple. You provided for them when their own resources failed. Your miracle of water made into wine sustained the celebration of the two people whose marriage You attended. We seek that same blessing and invite

Your presence now with us. Celebrate with us, as husbands and wives joined with one another in this group. Be here to help us, when we come short of supplying the needs of others. Transform our marriages and the business we transact in this gathering by making us aware that You are with us. Help us to share Your life with one another. Reveal Yourself again, especially where we recognize needs. We turn to You with trust and confidence, O Christ, our Lord. **Amen.**

Spirit of life, Your creative power shaped the world and gave life to the forms that were made. Your sanctifying grace brings life even where there is death. We thank You for the new life we enjoy in the relationship of husband and wife. We thank You for the creative power that is shared by fathers and mothers among us. We thank You for the gift of eternal life which we have received through the death and resurrection of Jesus Christ. Move in us and through us to others, as You did at Pentecost. As we speak with one another, let others hear of God's saving works. Show that You are present by the effects You have upon us. Make us alive in the flesh and powerful in spirit, so we can enjoy our time together. Help us to work and to plan confidently for the future. We ask this through Christ our Lord. **Amen.**

Father in heaven, You call people into Your kingdom and enrich their lives by letting them share love as husband and wife. Lead us closer to one another as we come close to You.

Son of God, You are the Word made flesh upon earth. In the everyday business of living we need Your presence. Make our ordinary days and familiar relationships special for us.

Holy Spirit, You alone can inspire and renew what we have taken for granted. Make us see how special You are and how special we can be to one another.

In this group we are ready to serve You and to help others. Direct our thoughts, so that our decisions and our projects please You and further our faith, individually and together. In the name of God: Father, Son, Holy Spirit. **Amen.**

MEN'S CLUB

Read: Ps. 34; Matt. 16:24-27; Rom. 12:1-4; 1 Thess. 4:9-12

Sing: Lord, keep us steadfast in Your Word or, Onward, Christian soldiers

Almighty God, all people have been created in Your image. You also give us special opportunities to reflect the image of Your Son in our dealings with others. Grant that we who are fathers may be as caring and guiding as You are, heavenly Father. Grant that we, as sons of our earthly fathers, may give pride and credit to them and to You, who have created us and made us as we are. Grant that we may so love those in our world that we are ready to give what is valuable and close to us in order to help them finally to enjoy eternal peace with You. In our circle of friends and fellow workers, make each of us a blessing to others and a strength for those in need. You are over all, and provide for all. So likewise direct those who are our leaders here, in order that we may do good to all men. In the name of Jesus. **Amen.**

Jesus Christ, our Savior, You came to earth as a man, to save and sanctify. Help us to understand the rich privilege You give us who are also men. Let Your image be better formed in us. Let us be a saving help to others, as You are. Forgive us when we imagine that to be a man we must be crude or overbearing or untouchable or distant. You are the most perfect of all men. You overcame the curse that came upon the world by the first man. You were willing to give of Yourself and to bear the sins of all. Make us men like You, with a proper kind of strength and a helpful attitude of concern. Make us manly in our faith, men of conscience and sensitivity. Guide our group in its discussions and works, to accomplish the Father's will, as You did, Christ our Lord. **Amen.**

Spirit of God, we are men of flesh and blood. But God breathed His breath into us, and we are living beings because of You. We begin our meeting in the name of Christ and as children of our heavenly Father. Restore to us the joy of Your salvation. Help us to talk together and work together in sincere harmony, as brothers together with Christ and with each other. Take away that false pride that isolates us from one another and refuses to share with honesty and love. Whatever work You give us to do, we will do it with all our might and the power which You supply. Give us those spiritual gifts which are appropriate and needed at this moment. Open to all of us here those doors through which You want us to pass. Make us all wise men who show by our lives that we worship Jesus. In His name we pray. **Amen.**

Father of light, every good and perfect gift comes from You. Let our light shine so that others may see our good works and glorify You.

Son of the Father, make us ready to do the will of our Father in heaven as You did. Give us Your approval and also receive us to eternal glory.

Spirit of God, proceeding from Father and Son, drive us to those tasks of ministry for which You have called us. Prepare us to serve God in all we do.

Great and loving God, unfold for us the mystery of Your presence and plan. Grant that we too may be a blessing to others and consider their well-being before our own. Grant that we may truly be men, for we ask it in Jesus' name. **Amen.**

MISSION SOCIETY

Read: Ps. 61; Matt. 10:26-33; Luke 9:1-6; 2 Thess. 3:1-5

Sing: All hail the power of Jesus' name or, You are the Way; to You alone

O God, because of Jesus Christ You receive us as Your dear children, in this life and the life to come. Because of Jesus Christ, we are ready to be sent, to strangers far off and to friends and family nearby. But we cannot come to You nor go as Your representatives unless You continue to accept and help us. So we pause now to acknowledge how much we need You. We confess how ready we are to rely on everyone and anything but You, in our work that brings glory to Your name. The sin from which You have saved us still threatens us. We are not yet free of the temptation to operate with our own resources and even with the methods of those who do not know You. Help us now, we pray, for the sake of Jesus Christ, so that we begin, continue, and end our work with total dependence upon You and with complete reliance that Your will shall be done. **Amen.**

Beautiful Savior, Jesus Christ, what else can we do but confess Your name? How else can we live except with constant praise to You? For

You redeemed us from death and damnation. Where else can we turn for help but to You? No one else can give us a love that overcomes fear and death and is great enough to save all. Yours is the only name, You are the only one, that brings salvation. We thank You for saving us and changing our lives now and forever. Your kindness and Your goodness transforms us into Your representatives. We praise You for uniting us to You and to one another eternally. Your gift makes us the family of God. We bless You for keeping us safe from present and future dangers. Your gracious power overcomes all evil. Make it so now, O Lord. We will follow You, and in Your name we will speak. **Amen.**

Holy Spirit, human understanding can never lead to faith in Jesus Christ. Human effort cannot cause a person to come to Him. Only as You call, gather, enlighten, and sanctify people can they become children of God and members of Your church. We have received these blessings. We thank You. We share them with believers everywhere. We pray You to keep us with Jesus Christ in the one true faith. Day after day forgive our sins and the sins of all believers. On the Last Day raise all the dead and give all believers in Christ eternal life. Convince us, O God, that this faith we confess is most certainly true. Give us words to speak so that others may hear and believe and be saved, through Jesus Christ. **Amen.**

God our Father, from eternity You are Lord and Ruler of all the nations. Give us the confidence that everything is in Your hands and under Your control, so we also may do Your will.

God the Son, in the fullness of time You lived and died and rose again to be Lord and Savior of all the nations. Give us love, so that like You we may be willing to give of ourselves for the salvation of others.

God, Holy Spirit, You create faith when and where You will. Give us wisdom and courage at this time, so that our words and witness may be beneficial to many.

God, our God, prevent us from keeping You to ourselves or from hiding You from others. You are God over all and Savior for all, through Jesus Christ. **Amen.**

A Litany

*(The leader will announce the
responses in advance)*

O Lord,
O Christ,
O Lord:
    HAVE MERCY ON US
For the good news of salvation,
For the messengers of peace,
For life and hope in Jesus:
    WE THANK YOU, LORD.
For opportunities to witness to Christ,
For forgiveness when we fail,

For eternal joy with those who believe:
    WE THANK YOU, LORD.
For those who go far off to preach,
For those with us who share the Gospel,
For young and old who witness gladly:
    WE THANK YOU, LORD.
We pray for all who are persecuted when they
       speak,
    for boldness to suffer when they are abused;
We pray for the many kinds of missionaries You
       send,
    for help in teaching and learning and sharing;
We pray for those who do not believe Your word,
    for conversion when they are hardened or
      afraid or unsure.
    Lord, in Your mercy:
    HEAR OUR PRAYER

Send us and others, so that all might be saved,
through Jesus Christ, our Lord. **Amen.**

Good and loving God, forgive us for the excuses we give to others because we do not love them enough. Forgive us for the excuses we offer to You why we cannot go and tell and gather others into Your kingdom. Forgive us for unwillingness to respond to Your invitation and to be gathered together with others who hear Your voice. Forgive us for times when we have denied our faith silently and out loud, when we were not witnesses to You or bearers of Your Gospel. Forgive us for carelessness and foolishness in dealing with others, who were then uncertain or turned away from You by our failures. Forgive us for pride and self-righteousness, which convinced others that they did not want to be children of God as we claimed to be. Forgive us, O God, for the sake of Jesus Christ. Now, forgiven, we go again in His name. **Amen.**

O God, is there no one who will listen? Is there no way to convince them? Is there no hope of their turning from sin? Is there no desire to be godly? Is there no hungering and thirsting after righteousness? Is there no sign of Your presence? Is there no time to explain? We are saddened and discouraged, for many do not know You and many deny You. We recognize the thousands and millions who are unsaved in our world today. We wonder whether we can have any effect on them. We doubt if they ever will believe, even if one were to rise from the dead. But You have risen, Lord Jesus. You are alive. You are with us. Even those who turn away from You will finally see You and confess You as Lord. So enable us now, by Your Spirit, to speak of what we believe. Grant that they too will believe, now, through Jesus Christ. **Amen.**

Send us, O Lord, for we are Your people. We will speak of You. Prepare us, O Lord, for we are weak. We cannot testify by ourselves. Accompany us, O Lord, for we cannot go alone. We are quickly turned aside.

Open our eyes and our hearts to see the many
who do not know You. Use our time and our offerings to bring others to You. Make us willing
and able to give our witness, so that they may be
saved.

You are all powerful: protect us from harm
and danger. You are all gracious: convince them
of sin and salvation. You are all wise: teach us
and everyone to fear and love and trust in You
more than anything else. Ever-present Lord, be
with us where we go. At the end bring us home
to You, for we pray in Jesus' name. **Amen.**

 **MOTHERS CLUB**

Read: Ps. 139:1-12; Luke 1:35-38; Gal. 4:22-28
Sing: My soul now magnifies the Lord or, Of the
Father's love begotten

God our Father, we are grateful that You are
a Father in heaven and have blessed us to be
mothers on earth. Together we bear and give life.
Together we raise and nourish children. Together
we are pleased when our work is successful.

We too are proud of our children. We ask You
in Your kindness: help them and us, forgive them
and us, keep them and us. In our personal lives
and in this group we carry out Your will when

You direct and correct us. We turn to You in our
need and believe that because of Your Son Jesus
You will make us good mothers.

Watch over us and all we do. May our work
be done well, for the sake of Jesus. **Amen.**

Lord Jesus, like Mary Your mother we have
been bearers of life. We too were kept in child-
birth and to this day. Our children have been a
precious trust from God which we have worked
to raise.

In our gathering now, we ask You to be present and helpful. We ask for Your attention and
interest in the way that You healed other women
and accepted their ministry in Your days on
earth. Take our plans and wishes and use them
in ways that are pleasing and proper to You.

Bless our children. Show us how to help them
and when to stand aside, so they know they are
loved and can learn to be individuals too. Give us
the same attitude toward those with whom we
meet and work. Let everyone of us be all that we
can be, all that You want us to be.

Forgive us, as You did Mary at the wedding
in Cana, when we try to tell You what to do. But
provide for us, as You did for her at Your cross.
Amen.

Holy Spirit of God, You overshadowed the Virgin Mary. She conceived and bore a Son. We
remember how Your power also created and preserved life in us when we became mothers. Re-

mind us that we too are handmaidens of the Lord, and He has regarded and exalted us.

Our souls rejoice in God, our Savior. He is mighty and has done great things for us. Holy is His name. We respond to Your grace by our life and work together here. We ask You to help us in the program that we consider at this time.

Show us that our work is pleasing and valuable in Your sight. Help us to believe that it is not in vain in the Lord. Keep us from disagreements and disharmony, from arguments and anger. Let our spirits be calm and peaceful. In Jesus' name. **Amen.**

Mighty Lord, You are all in all. Be in us today, and the life we live will be Yours.

Lord Jesus, You are with us always. Speak to us today, and the words we say will be Yours.

Holy Spirit of God, You fill the world. Inspire us today, and our actions will be Yours.

O God, we are sisters of Jesus Christ, our elder Brother. We are sisters in the flesh with all women who bear life and bring it to the Lord. According to Your will, use us and what we do here as a life-giving force for others. Remove all evil from us. Turn the power of death away from us.

In You we live and move and have our being. And so do our children. And so do all people. We thank You for that knowledge and faith, through Christ, the Lord. **Amen.**

OUTDOOR MEETING

Read: Ps. 8 or 19:1-6; Rom. 8:18-25
Sing: Abide with me, fast falls the eventide or,
Now the day is over

Almighty God, we praise You for the marvels of nature and the delights of creation. We too are fearfully and wonderfully made, by Your design, a little lower than the angels. We thank You for Your creative goodness and revealed power. You also lowered Yourself to human existence in the person of Your Son, Jesus Christ. He is the new Adam and Creator of a new humanity. Send Your Spirit who moved on the face of the water. Send Your life-giving breath to fill us, newly made and open to Your presence. We shall never cease thanking You for being a God who creates and preserves life. We acknowledge that You are our God and we are Your people. Accept our praise, because of the intercession of Jesus Christ, our Lord. **Amen.**

O God, in the beginning You created heaven and earth. Now You have created us also. You have given us body and soul and all our being. Daily and richly You provide us with all we need. In this outdoor setting we can observe Your good world and also see the damage done to it by the sins of mankind. Let the beauty of Your redeeming love in Jesus Christ overcome the ravages of evil. We confess that this is our Father's world. We know that we have been placed here to care for it and to enjoy it. Teach us to appreciate the natural blessings we have, tokens of the supernatural riches You promise to us in Your Son. Forgive us for carelessness and mistreatment of natural resources. Forgive us for the destruction and harm we cause by our poor care of creation. Forgive us for treating Your world as if it were meant for us alone to possess. We look forward to a new heaven and a new earth, even as we now live and serve You in this world through Christ our Lord. **Amen.**

PARENT-TEACHER ORGANIZATION

Read: Ps. 111; Matt. 5:17-20; Acts 18:24-28
Sing: To God the Holy Spirit let us pray or, Just as I am, without one plea

Dear Father in heaven, You have entrusted children to us as precious gifts. We thank You for the joy they bring to us, their parents and teachers. Help us to provide them with care and good training. Bless us with the resources to provide for their physical and spiritual needs and for their eternal well-being. We begin in fear of You, recognizing the responsibility You have given to us. We continue by Your grace and support, with help from Your Word and from one another. We rest all our hope in Your love, trusting that You will use our efforts for the well-being of our school and students. We pray that our efforts to train our children in the way they should go will result in adults who do not depart from You. Teach us how to do that, O God, through Your Son Jesus. **Amen.**

Lord Jesus, we and the children for whose good we meet today have been baptized. We are Your disciples. We want to teach them all that You have commanded us. We ask that You be with us always. By using Your Word, the inspired record of Your teaching to others, help us to be good teachers and parents. Make us sensitive to each individual, as You are. Turn us from impersonal and uncaring decisions for the lives of these young people. We meet because we can help each other. We plan and discuss because we need each other. We pray now because all our efforts will fail unless You are the center of all we do. You were called Rabbi and Teacher in the days of Your earthly ministry. People received wisdom from You. We seek the same gift, in Your name. **Amen.**

Spirit of wisdom and truth, lead us and remind us of all that Jesus said and did. We ask for Your inspiration in the work we do in our school and in this organization. Protect us from false wisdom, the wisdom of this world, that does not know You nor the Father nor His Son. Increase our wisdom, so we enjoy favor with God and man. Inspire us to attempt great things, to the glory of our Father and for the benefit of our students and children. We recognize that we have different viewpoints and outlooks in our separate roles as parents and teachers, but we are united in love for our children. Give us unity and harmony. Use us to correct and teach one another. Come, Holy Spirit, fill our hearts and our minds now, in the name of Jesus. **Amen.**

Father, our children were baptized to be Your children too. Grant that they and we may speak to You with confidence and trust.

Jesus, our children believe in You also. Grant that we and they may follow You in each day's life and actions.

Spirit, our children were given true life by Your calling. Grant that they and we may live and do the good works which You have ordained for us.

God, Father, Son, and Spirit, our children must grow more and more to know You, to imitate You, and to depend on You. Grant that we and they may begin and end each day with an increase of faith and hope and love.

Let us grow in grace, parents and teachers and children alike, for Jesus' sake. **Amen.**

A Litany

*(The leader will announce the
reponses in advance)*

O Lord,
O Christ,
O Lord:
    HAVE MERCY ON US.
For parents, responsible for lives of the young,
For teachers, helpers, and guides to students,
For children, alive in Christ through us:
    WE THANK YOU, LORD.
For faith, without which we cannot please You,
For knowledge, to learn Your marvelous ways,
For wisdom, to use what we know and believe:
    WE THANK YOU, LORD.
For those who preceded us, and prepared the way
        for us,
For those who follow us, and benefit from our
        work,
For those who are here now, and help one another
        grow:
    WE THANK YOU, LORD.
We pray for bright and gifted students,
    that they may use their talents well;
We pray for slow and troubled learners,
    that they may persevere and succeed;
We pray for average and steady children,
    that they strive for excellence and overcome
        limits:
    Lord, in Your mercy:
    HEAR OUR PRAYER.

Hear us and help us, to grow in fear and love and trust in You, by knowing Jesus Christ, whom You sent for our eternal life. **Amen.**

God, our Father, we are thankful that You have richly blessed our lives, our homes, and our schools. We thank You for the privilege of teaching Your children to know You and to place their trust in You. Keep us from carelessness in our tasks. Show us how to instruct and admonish the children. Teach us also how to comfort and encourage them. Help us to be good examples to students and to one another, so they may grow in faith and joy. Make children obedient to parents and teachers. Make teachers and parents considerate of children. Guard these Your children. In mercy, let none of them stray from the truth in their earthly life. Help us to recognize both the responsibilities and opportunities we have to serve You and our children. Give us a comprehensive view of education, mindful of mental, physical, emotional, and social factors as well as spiritual well-being. We ask this through our divine Teacher, Jesus Christ. **Amen.**

PLANNING COMMITTEE

Read: Ps. 91; Luke 16:10-13; 1 Cor. 3:5-9; 2 Cor. 6:1-10
Sing: Lift high the cross, the love of Christ proclaim or, With the Lord begin your task

Heavenly Father, Your mercy and grace have made us members of Your church and kingdom. We gather now to plan for the future and to organize our work. We seek a way that pleases You and carries out Your will among us. Give us unity of heart and mind to consider the tasks and challenges of our church here and elsewhere. Give us clear perspective on present matters along with a vision of what can be done. Open our imaginations to anticipate the course of our church in the coming months, so we may plan and prepare for what lies ahead. Give us the will and wisdom to share our convictions and our enthusiasm with those who follow our leadership. Above all, grant us the teaching and leading of Your Holy Spirit. His power will assure that we believe Your Holy Word and live a godly life, on earth now and in heaven forever. Let Your kingdom come, through Christ our Lord. **Amen.**

Lord, we pause at the start of this planning session to recall Your purposes in this world. Those You foreknew You predestined to be conformed to the likeness of Your Son. Those You called, You also justified. Those You justified, You also glorified. You did not spare Your own Son, but gave Him up for us all. You will also, along with Him, give us all things. We are therefore more than conquerors through Your love. Nothing will be able to separate us from Your love in Christ Jesus our Lord. For Your saving plan and action, we praise You. We resolve to carry out the assignments given to us in the same manner as You have dealt with us. Help us, heavenly Father, to proceed now, grateful for Your blessing and mindful of Your guidance. Help us to serve You well, in the name of Jesus. **Amen.**

SCOUT TROOP MEETING

Read: Ps. 92; Rom. 12:9-13; Gal. 4:25-29; Eph. 4:1-6; Phil. 4:4-9; 2 Tim. 2:1-7

Sing: God bless our native land or, O Lord, my God, when I in awesome wonder

Lord Jesus Christ, we come together now in Your name for our scout meeting and activities. We ask for Your presence and blessing. Grant that the knowledge and skills we develop here may be useful to other people and to our community. We want to glorify You and let our light shine. Keep us pure in heart, upright in life, diligent in all our work, and gifted with every Christian virtue. We look to You as the author and finisher of our faith. In Your name we begin, continue, and complete our tasks. Give us joy and benefit from our being together. Increase our skills and abilities. Prepare us to be useful adults. Instruct and direct our leaders to do the same for us. We ask this in Your name. **Amen.**

Almighty God and Father, we recall how You led and trained the people of Israel during their exodus from slavery. You went with them on their travels through the desert until they reached the promised land where they were to settle. Direct and bless us, as we move forward into new areas of service and skill. Teach us what we need to know in order to carry out Your will in our lives and the lives of others. Train us for our future lives. Equip us to handle the responsibilities that will be ours. Let each award we receive and each objective we complete on the way to our goals be a sign of that eternal reward that awaits us, not by our own good works but completely through the merits of Your Son, Jesus Christ. In His name we bring our prayers to You. **Amen.**

SCOUT CAMP SERVICE

God of our fathers, Lord of our salvation, the heavens declare Your glory and the earth demonstrates Your marvelous creation. In this outdoor setting we remember that You placed Adam and Eve within the garden to care for what You had made. Your creation was given to them to enjoy. Not even their sin, nor ours, can completely remove the many signs of Your grace and blessing. They surround us as we gather in this place to worship You. Your grace kept Your people safe in their travels through the world under Your direction. We seek that same grace, so that we too may know that You are near in love as well as power. Show us that You want to redeem us as well as to rule us. In the silence and the sounds of our solemn service, we come in Spirit and in truth to You, through Christ our Lord. **Amen.**

O God, we know that You are here. We confess that You are near. We recognize the signs of Your presence in the wonders of nature that surround us. When we consider the sun, the moon, and the stars, we wonder why You also care for us. In the trees, the flowers, the grass, we see proof of Your providence and protection. By Your command, the rain falls on good and bad

alike. The sun shines on the righteous and unrighteous. We cannot know or understand all the
mysteries of the universe. We feel small and in-
significant at the size and power of all that You
have made. We can only offer You praise and
thanks for letting us enjoy these good things. We
pray for You to be with us now and always. Keep
us from danger. Make us glad to belong to You.
Bless our worship, in the name of Jesus. **Amen.**

STEWARDSHIP COMMITTEE

Read: Ps. 41 or 49; Mark 10:23-31; 2 Tim.
2:20-26
Sing: Let me be Yours forever or, Lord of glory,
You have bought us

Almighty Father, all the wealth of heaven and
earth is Yours. You are Creator, Ruler, and
Giver of all. We appreciate that You lend these
gifts to us during our time on earth. Whatever
we give is being returned to You. Receive our
offerings of hand and heart. Make them eternally
valuable by Your blessing. Teach us to live with
an awareness that You are in all that we do. Help
us to feel compassion for those in need by every
work and deed and thought of our lives. By Your
Holy Spirit, move all who live to live in love, until

You greet in heaven all who have lived on earth as Your sons and daughters. In Your great generosity You give us the model and the means to be generous to others. We see Your grace especially in the gift of Your Son Jesus Christ, to be our Savior and Redeemer. By His intercession hear and answer our prayers. Make us good managers in Your world. **Amen.**

Savior Jesus Christ, You cared so well for all that the Father placed into Your hands during Your life on earth. You wasted nothing. You lost no one of all that were committed to Your care. No one was too small or too great to receive Your attention. You used them all to the glory of Him who sent You. We ask You now to help us to develop and carry out that kind of stewardship for what our Father gives us. Do not let us yield to the temptation to be selfish or greedy. Do not allow actual needs in our own lives to cancel out awareness of the needs of others. Do not permit the luxuries we enjoy to be gained at the expense of someone else's well-being. We want to love people, because You did. We want to use things because You have shared them with us. Forgive us when we use people because we love things too much. You are our Lord. Rule us. **Amen.**

Spirit of God, You create a bond of fellowship and support by Your gifts to us. We have been warned by the fate of Ananias and Sapphira. We want to be honest with You in reviewing our performance and sharing with others. We are not ready to surrender everything we have, and we admit it. We ask You by Your holy inspiration to make us more generous and more giving day by day. We give You thanks and praise for the freedom to decide how we will distribute the many resources at our disposal. Forgive when we decide badly and improperly. Open our hearts and lives to Your indwelling. Shape us into the vessels of glory to convey Your riches to others. Inspire us, we pray. Then we will teach transgressors Your ways and sinners will be converted to You, for Jesus' sake. **Amen.**

STUDENT GROUP

Read: Ps. 121; Luke 14:25-33; Rom. 13:8-10
Sing: Awake, Thou Spirit of the watchmen or, Glory be to God the Father

We remember You now, Creator, in the days of our youth. We have learned much and received much from those who taught us. We know that there is much more to find and to know. We believe that we are Your beloved children and disciples of Your Son Jesus Christ. Your Spirit speaks in our hearts. Draw us closer to You and to the perfection that You have planned for us.

In our study and recreation, teach us to recognize Your presence and providence. In times of stress and anxiety, convince us that You are our hope in years to come and have been our help in the past. By our quiet reflection and active recreation, give us true gladness at the opportunity to show You to others in every phase of our lives. Open our hearts to see those around us that we can help. When we are nearer to You than they are, show us how we can help them. We ask in Jesus' name. **Amen.**

Lord Jesus, we consider the mystery of Your incarnation. You too had to increase in wisdom and in stature and in favor with God and men. We are flesh and blood as You were then. We ask for Your guidance and help as we pursue a fuller education and continued growth. When questions come which challenge our faith, assure us that You are our Wisdom. When answers are given that conflict with our belief, give us good judgment and patience to resolve the tension. We are thankful for this time and place to come together in Christian fellowship and worship. Our lives and our gathering are incomplete without You. Come to us with blessing, for we wait for You in Word and Sacrament. Go with us as we leave this place. Convince us that we are never alone. Let all we do, like this prayer, be in Your name. **Amen.**

Spirit of God, when we cannot express ourselves, You carry our petitions to the Father.

Since we often leave the way God has planned for us, You come to us with the saving presence of Christ. For Your constant, mothering compassion and care, we give You thanks and praise. In times past You inspired others of the faithful to speak Your message, to bear God's grace, and to resist and conquer evil. Grant us those same gifts. Use us in the same way You have used others. Then Your name will be holy, Your kingdom will come, and Your will be done. Show us that we are more grown up than our parents think and less grown up than we imagine. Help us to be what we are and what You have made us to be, rather than what the world wants to make us. Hear us in the name of Christ. **Amen.**

SUNDAY SCHOOL CONFERENCE

Read: Ps. 1 or 142; Matt. 18:10-14; Luke 2:41-52; Luke 24:13-27; Acts 8:25-35; Titus 3:8-11

Sing: We praise You, O God or, Holy God, we praise Your name or, Holy Spirit, light divine

O Lord, we have all been taught by You. We know You and Jesus Christ. Now we come together at this conference to share the wisdom and understanding given to each one. We pray that all will benefit by a fuller revelation of Your will and ways. Give us harmony and good will, to participate actively in the events that have been planned. Help us to avoid that false wisdom which the world claims to possess. Do not let us boast of our wisdom, but let us rejoice in the Lord. We want to receive and to impart to our students and co-workers the spirit of Your Son, who came from You to claim us as Your own people. Give us open hearts and honest mouths. Make us quick to hear, slow to speak, slow to anger. Be with us now, in the name of our Lord Jesus Christ. **Amen.**

Lord, our Father, we gather together in Your name. We have come from many places and with a variety of needs. We want to feed and to be nourished. We want to teach and to learn. Our mutual concerns bind us by necessity. Our shared faith unites us in love. Let the example of the early Christians provide us with direction and encouragement, so that we too may conclude our conference in a way that pleases You. As You guide us, we declare that it seems good to the Holy Spirit and to us to proceed as we shall decide. We covet boldness of speech, to carry the Gospel of Your Son to others. Grant us such a wealth of Your Spirit that we powerfully demonstrate our convictions with more than just word and speech. We know the Scriptures and the power You have. Keep us in them and free from error, for the sake of Jesus Christ. **Amen.**

SUNDAY SCHOOL SESSION

Heavenly Father, we thank You for revealing Yourself to us as a good and gracious Lord. We praise You for giving Your written Word to speak to us today. We thank You for teachers and leaders in our Sunday school, who serve You and lead us into all the truth. Grant that all of us, young and old, men and women, boys and girls, teachers and students, may glorify You in our worship, our study, and our discussion. Be present with those who are absent today, especially those who are kept away by sickness or other problems at home. Reward the parents and church members who give their support to the operation of our Sunday school and the well-being of all who attend. Direct our Sunday school, those of other churches, and those in far-off lands. Let people and children everywhere hear Your Gospel and be saved, through Jesus Christ. **Amen.**

Lord Jesus, our Redeemer, we thank You for saving us by Your cross and resurrection. We are glad to know Your love and Your desire to be with us. Keep us safe now and forever. Be in our midst as we gather in Your name. Welcome us to Your eternal home to be with You forever when we come to the place that You have prepared for us in heaven. We come to Your Father's house to discuss the Scriptures, to ask and to answer questions, and to learn Your will for our lives. We will be pleased if others are amazed at our learning. But we will be even happier if You will open the Scriptures to us. In the psalms and the law and the prophets we want to find You and the Father's will for all people. We will follow You and we will learn from You, for You are our Lord and Savior. **Amen.**

Spirit and lord, we cannot believe in Jesus Christ our Lord by our own understanding or effort. We need You to call us through the Gospel, to enlighten us with Your gifts, to sanctify and keep us in true faith. And You call, gather, enlighten, and sanctify the whole Christian church on earth and keep it with Jesus Christ in the one true faith. Today and every day forgive us our sins. On the Last Day raise up all the dead and give all believers in Christ eternal life. Until that final resurrection, nourish and increase the life of Christ in us, make us joyful and certain in our faith. Lead us into God's Word for help. Lead us through all the trials of life. Grant that we do not fall into disbelief, despair, and other great shame or failing. Satisfy our thirst for knowledge with the water of life that comes from Jesus Christ, our Lord. **Amen.**

Almighty Father, we come as Your dear children. We pray that You will guide us into Your Word and protect us from all harm.

Lord Jesus, we pray to You as our Savior and Brother. We ask that You will forgive our sins and make us more like You.

Holy Spirit, we seek Your help as God and Lord. Give us the spiritual gifts we need to serve You.

O God, we thank You for being our God, for sharing Your life with us and for being willing to come and help us. Keep us from the temptations to be disrespectful and disobedient while we are being taught. Keep us from the temptations to be harsh and unfair when we teach. Give us an understanding of what You say to us. Help us develop readiness to apply Your Word to ourselves before we use it to judge others. Be present for our good and Your glory, in Jesus' name. **Amen.**

A Litany

(The leader will announce the responses in advance)

O Lord,
O Christ,
O Lord:
   HAVE MERCY ON US.
For teachers and students and helpers,
For books and pictures and aids,
For worship and study and projects:
   WE THANK YOU, LORD.
For the Bible, the book of life,
For prayer, our help in need,
For the world, the place where we are:

WE THANK YOU, LORD.
For words of teaching, to instruct us in truth,
For silence, to think about Your love,
For activity, to practice what we teach:
    WE THANK YOU, LORD.
We pray for those who are here and well. Give
    us a blessing in this time.
We pray for all who are absent and sick,
Give them healing and help their need.
We pray for the lost who are distant from You.
    Give them direction and reason to come.
Lord, in Your mercy:
    HEAR OUR PRAYER.

Bless us all in the time we share and give us good times and pleasant memories, until we are eternally with You, through Jesus our Lord. **Amen.**

We pray, O God, that You will make us able to teach and willing to learn. Clear our minds from thinking those thoughts that are displeasing to You. Take away thoughts of things that interfere with receiving Your Word. We come to this place today from our own homes and lives. Join us together in spirit and thought. Make us united in Christ. Let each of us find a way to contribute to others. Make us ready to offer whatever we have that can make someone else's life richer and happier. Do not let us despise the little ones who believe in You. Do not let us neglect Your Word and the teaching of it. Make us Your kind of people. We gladly hear and learn what You say and do. We call on You in every trouble. We pray, praise, and give You thanks in the name of Jesus. **Amen.**

SUNDAY SCHOOL TEACHERS MEETING

God, our Father, to teach others about You is an awesome and almost overwhelming task. We are humbled and frightened by knowing that we teachers shall be judged more strictly than others. Such warnings confuse and discourage us. Do not let us rely on our own efforts to be good teachers. In our emptiness and weariness, come to us with Your grace and power. Let our sufficiency be from You. Fill us, so that we can give to others. Use us in Your own way. We await Your saving and creative touch. We pause now before we begin to do our work this day. Work in us again and make us ready for the time when You will work through us. We know we can trust You to hear us and to help, by the intercession of Your Son, our Lord Jesus Christ. **Amen.**

Lord Jesus, You were happy when children came to You. You took them up in Your arms, put Your hands upon them and blessed them. Today we are Your hands. We want to bless the children who come to You when they come to us for teaching and training. Prepare us in whatever way You choose, to be able to carry out our assignments as You have done. We follow You and listen to Your voice now. We speak to one another and listen to the message of Your Word in Holy Scripture. Give us the faith of little children, so we can believe what You say. Give us the understanding of mature adults, so we can explain it to others. Comfort us now and in our classes and other duties by being with us, whatever we are doing. We need You every hour. We want You to be with us at all times, O Lord, our Savior. **Amen.**

Lord, Holy Spirit, only You can search the deep things of God and reveal them to us. Only You can teach us to convey spiritual truths in spiritual words and to spiritual people. In times past You spoke by the prophets. Today we have the privilege of being used by You. Give us a spirit of harmony and cooperation throughout our Sunday school, especially among all of us who teach together. Drive out all evil. Fill us with Yourself. Let no demons return to control us and what we do. When we cannot understand or control our students, help us to love and accept them. Convince us that we are special and privileged workers in Your kingdom. Do not let us feel sorry for ourselves but only for those who do not know You.

Help us to teach well, for the sake of Jesus Christ. **Amen.**

Father, You spoke and it was done. By Your Word everything in heaven and earth came into being.

Son of God, You are the Word made flesh. In You dwells the whole fullness of God.

Holy Spirit, You guarantee that the Word will not return void and without effect. God will accomplish His will, as He says.

Speak to us, O God, in Your wonderful works and ways. Send us Your truth and grace, by Your beloved Son. Keep us silent and listening to Jesus; then open our lips so that our mouths may declare Your praise.

We thank You for calling us to this ministry of teaching in the Sunday school. Equip us to share Your Word with others. Give us a special blessing here at this meeting. Let our planning and preparation together bring a special blessing to those we teach. In Jesus' name. **Amen.**

WOMEN'S MISSIONARY GUILD OR LEAGUE

Read: Ps. 141; Matt. 10:40-42; John 3:16-21; Acts 8:34-43

Sing: Songs of thankfulness and praise or, How sweet the name of Jesus sounds

Lord, we come to You with our prayers and praise. We ask, "What do You want us to do?" We promise, "As for me and my house, we will serve the Lord." We are ready: "Here am I, send me." Show us where we can go and what You want us to do, Lord. We are Your servants and we will obey Your commands. Through others who came in Your name and brought Your saving Gospel to us, we have become Your people. We are heirs of heaven. Do not let us hoard or hide the gift of eternal life. Open our lives and our mouths to those who do not know You. We give glory to Your most holy name. We unworthy sinners have received mercy. We have a calling to represent You to others. Send us, O Lord, to every place where You Yourself will come with saving grace, in Jesus Christ. **Amen.**

Jesus of Nazareth, You are the Son of David and Lord of the nations. Ever since You called Your first diciples to follow You and to learn of God, You have prepared people to represent You. It helps us to know that You have been given all power in heaven and on earth. We are comforted by our belief that You are with us always, even to the close of the age. Now we are ready to learn of Your mission in the world today. We want to discover our place in Your total plan. Teach us the truth that You died to give us. Show us the Father who raised You from the dead. Give us Your Spirit, so we may do the works that You did. Let us imitate Your apostles in serving You. Mighty and ascended Lord, send us with Your blessing and direction. Call us together again to prepare to do more work. Be with us now. Be with us always, for You are Christ, the Lord. **Amen.**

Holy Spirit, having Jesus as our Savior gives us all that we need in this life and in the life to come. Strengthen our faith. Increase our love and hope. Add to our ability to know and to serve You. Give us grace to make progress in sanctified living. Keep us from whatever displeases You. Give us increase in good works. Direct our conduct and confession, our life and lips. Let us show in greater measure the glory of our eternally blessed Redeemer. Begin now, as we meet here today. Draw out those ideas and works which are in our hearts and minds. Nurture them so they develop into plans and projects. Finally crown them with Your blessing. Grant victories and accomplishments in accord with Your plans for salvation. Hear us for Jesus' sake. **Amen.**

Father in heaven, we lift up our hearts and voices in praise of You. We give thanks for all the saints of past and present who have served You and proclaimed salvation to others.

Jesus, God's Son, we add our joyful thanks to You. You endorsed the ministry of all who offered help, even with a cup of cold water or a kind word.

Holy Spirit, the gladness we express in our worship is the echo of Your powerful breath of salvation, which moves and inspires and gives true life to all.

God, Father, Son, and Holy spirit, we adore and worship You in our meeting. We praise You daily, one and all of us, with angels and archangels and all the company of heaven. Accept our offerings and everything we give You. Turn them into blessings for others, through Jesus Christ, the only Savior. **Amen.**

A Litany

*(The leader will announce the responses
in advance)*

O Lord,
O Christ,
O Lord:
HAVE MERCY ON US.
For all the people who represent You,
For every man who accepted responsibility,

For every woman who shared the task:
    WE THANK YOU, LORD.
For little gifts that help some way,
For mighty deeds that impress everyone,
For daily opportunity to do Your will:
    WE THANK YOU, LORD.
We pray for Christians safe in Your love, to be
          eternally saved by You.
We pray for unbelievers who have not heard, to
          be confronted with Your Good News.
We pray for people who doubt and forget, to be
          remembered by You in grace.
    Lord, in Your mercy:
    HEAR OUR PRAYER

    Send us with gladness and charity in Your
name, with heart and soul and body dedicated to
Your service and redeemed by Your Son, Jesus
Christ, our Lord. **Amen.**

God of all, raise our sights and increase our
vision. We come together today in Your name
to respond to Your command to be Your missionaries. By Your help we can see and reach the
many who have yet to experience the joy of salvation in Christ. By Your encouragement we can
accept and believe the plans You have for saving
others. By Your guidance we can develop and
carry out those strategies and programs that
mean eternal life to those who still live without
hope. We thank You that with our Christian sisters we can be part of that movement which de-

stroys the power of sin and death in the world and brings relief to those who suffer from evil. Bless and unite us with all Your people. Make us an effective force throughout the world and let our witness reach to the heavens. We ask it through Him who was sent and now sends, Jesus Christ our Lord. **Amen.**

YOUNG ADULTS/SINGLES

Read: Ps. 110; Luke 7:11-17; 1 Cor. 7:25-31; Col. 3:12-17

Sing: All depends on our possessing or, All who would valiant be

God, our Father, we dedicate ourselves anew to You and to Your will for us. By Your kind direction we are here together. We are united in love and devotion to You. Share with us Your Spirit's power. Let us pursue Your purpose and pleasure in all that we plan and do together. Give us ingenuity and creativity in doing new and good things for You and for one another. Extend our service beyond our own organization. Let us benefit strangers and outsiders who are looking for signs of Your rule and control in the world and in their lives. Make us bold for the sake of Your church. Further our fellowship with one another.

Help us to deepen our relationships. Increase our support for one another. Give us a view of what we are doing that includes what You want done by us. Remind us of those who are younger and those who are older than we are. Make us ready to do good to all, especially those who are of the household of faith. For we pray in Jesus' name. **Amen.**

Lord Jesus Christ, God and man, we recall now that You were once a young adult. You too were single when God appointed You to carry out His saving will. We give You thanks for Your sacrificial offering for us and for all people. Now we are saved. We have been given an example of service which we can to some extent imitate. We can never be all that You are. We can never do all that You do. We can do more than we have done. We can glorify our Father by our thoughts and words and actions. Help us to accomplish some of the saving work that remains to be done. We are willing to share the sufferings which You have endured. May each of us and all of us together find power and peace in Your name, Lord Jesus Christ. **Amen.**

Mighty and gracious Spirit of God, in times past You inspired God's people to act in His name and to carry out His will. As we come together in this group now, we are aware of our deficiencies and our needs. Forgive us for what is past which grieved You. We also recognize the potential and possibilities that are before us because You lead us in faith. Give us a readiness to respond to every opportunity to do God's work in our time. Fill us and our gathering with an atmosphere of unity and peace. Let us proceed with cooperation and openness. Take away the fear of others, which keeps us from sharing our gifts with them. Temper the impatience with others, which prevents them from working for the common good. In this crucial time, use our childhood experiences to prepare us to live in full maturity, as sons and daughters of God. Hear us and grant our prayers, through Christ our Lord. **Amen.**

Lord God, rule us when we rebel. Impose Your will upon us when we are inclined to evil. Correct us when we err. Discipline us when we are careless.

Lord Jesus Christ, enrich our humanity by Your holy love. Raise us to spiritual excellence by forgiveness and mercy. Be with us always.

Lord Holy Spirit, share with us the riches which have been prepared for us. Give us love, joy, peace, patience, kindness, goodness, faithfulness, gentleness, self-control.

Almighty and loving Father, Son, and Spirit, reveal Your mystery in grace to us. Help us to understand the mystery of life and to follow those ways which are pleasing to You and good for us. Be present for us in every trouble. Share our gladness. Excite us with the awareness of what can be, through Your leadership and our cooperation. We ask this through Christ, our Lord. **Amen.**

YOUTH GROUP

Read: Ps. 8 or 29; Luke 10:21-24; 1 Cor. 6:17-20;
Eph. 4:11-16; 1 Tim. 4:12-16
Sing: Baptized into Your name most holy or,
Now rest beneath night's shadow

O Lord God, we do not want to be called children anymore. Yet we are pleased to be Your children. We know that we are growing in faith and good works. But we are impatient with ourselves because we do not do better. Use our meeting today to bless us with Your goodness. When we leave make us glad that we have been together. Help us to enjoy our time together. Control the temptations to do wrong that come to us. Give us the proper respect and attitude toward one another as brothers and sisters in Christ. Do not let us hurt one another or threaten another person's faith by our words or actions. We thank You for pastors and leaders and helpers, who join with us in meetings and activities. Show us how to express our appreciation to them. Give them satisfaction with what they accomplish with us. All this we ask in Jesus' name. **Amen.**

D ear Jesus, when You lived on earth as a human, You were once our age. You thought and felt and behaved as one of us. We are grateful that You shared this time of life that we are in now. You were tempted, as we are. But You did not sin, and we do. Our first need is for Your forgiveness. We ask You now to remove the load of guilt and sin that we bring with us today. We remember and confess the sins we have done. But we are tempted to relive them and to look forward to the next opportunity to commit them again. We admit that like Paul we often do the evil things we don't want to do. Just as often we don't do the good things we want to do. Deliver us from this bondage and death. Thanks to God, who gives us the victory through You, our Lord Jesus Christ. **Amen.**

Holy Spirit of God, the Virgin Mary was very much like one of us. You overshadowed her and used her to be the mother of our Savior Jesus Christ. Use us to carry Him into the world where we live and act today. Give the benefits of Your saving work to the people we know. We open ourselves to Your leading. We ask You to come and to be within us in all our business and in all our recreation. Remind us that our bodies are Your temples. Convince us that we are called to glorify God in our bodies and in our spirits. Show us that we have the mind of Christ. Help us together to think and to plan what makes for everyone's good. Give our leaders a sensitivity to the least of us. Make them able to control and direct us as pleases You. We pray that You will come to us, in the name of Jesus. **Amen.**

Father in heaven, we are Your sons and daughters. We have been baptized into Your name. We come with confidence and believe that You will hear us.

Jesus our Lord, we were buried with You in our baptism. We have died to sin. Teach us how to be alive to righteousness.

Holy Spirit, by the washing of regeneration You have renewed us. Be merciful to us. Because we are justified by Your grace, make us heirs in hope of eternal life.

O God of Trinity, drown our sinful self with all its evil deeds and desires, through daily repentance on our part. Raise up our new selves each day, to live with You in righteousness and purity forever. As Christ was raised from death by the glory of the Father, help us walk in newness of life. We pray in Christ our Lord. **Amen.**

A Litany

(The leader will announce the responses in advance)

O Lord, we come to You for mercy and for help:
    WE NEED YOUR HELP, O LORD.
To assist in keeping our young people in the fellowship of Your church:
    WE NEED YOUR HELP, O LORD.
To promote growth among all youth in understanding and use of Your Word:
    WE NEED YOUR HELP, O LORD.
To assist one another in preparation for a life of service to You and mankind:

WE NEED YOUR HELP, O LORD.
To develop an active love for the announcement
of forgiveness through Christ to all near at
hand and afar off:
WE NEED YOUR HELP, O LORD.
To foster godliness and true enjoyment in our so-
cial life and recreation:
WE NEED YOUR HELP, O LORD.
To encourage gifts and acts of service to all less
fortunate than ourselves:
WE NEED YOUR HELP, O LORD.
To build close ties and deep loyalties to our Chris-
tian homes:
WE NEED YOUR HELP, O LORD.
To guide one another through organized youth
activities in our congregation:
WE NEED YOUR HELP, O LORD.
To unite all youth who love You, the only true
God, and Jesus Christ, whom You have
sent:
WE NEED YOUR HELP, O LORD.

O Lord God, You know us as we are. You see
us as we can be. We ask Your help and blessing to bring the good things You intend for us into
reality. Some say we are too young, and we must
wait until we are adults. We believe that no one
should despise our youth and that we can be examples to other believers. Some say we are too
old, and we have lost the innocence of childhood.
We confess that we still have childlike faith in You
and in Your Son Jesus Christ, our Savior. Help

us to be mature in knowledge and in actions and to overcome what is childish about ourselves. Keep us trusting and obedient, able to avoid those errors that we so dislike in adults. Give us peace and cooperation with our parents and our leaders. Help us understand that all Your children are called to be saints. Hear us for the sake of Your Son, our Lord, Jesus Christ. **Amen.**

Heavenly Father, we thank You for this good time of our life. We thank You for all the possibilities that lie before us as we proceed with Your blessing. We pray for Your help in bad times of our life. Give us freedom from the guilt and shame that lie heavy upon us now from sins of the past. Come to us in grace. We pray that with hope and confidence we may look ahead and work for the well-being and improvement of everyone in our group. Come to us with power. Let the Spirit You placed in us at our baptism guide our thinking and planning and working. Give us worthwhile projects to do. Give us enjoyment in doing them together. Open the eyes and hearts of our church leaders and fellow members to accept what we are contributing to the life of this congregation. All our lives are in Your keeping. Keep us safe and close to You, for Christ's sake. **Amen.**

Almighty God, You claimed and supported Your Son when He came into this world. With Your voice You approved Him at His baptism. Help us to hear Your voice accepting and strengthening us. Do not forsake us because of our sin. For Jesus' sake cleanse us and restore us to Your holy family. Be our Father, especially when our parents fail us or we disappoint them. Be our Brother, when our brothers and sisters and those in our church family do not accept us. Be our God, when we decide to go our own way or fail to seek Your will in our lives. Be our inspiration, when our hopes seem unreal and we are discouraged. Be with us now and forever, so we may always be with You. In the name of Jesus. **Amen.**

YOUTH GROUP OUTDOOR MEETING

*(A personal prayer on behalf
of each individual)*

O Lord, my God, being here teaches me more about Your power and goodness than I can learn in a classroom. Feeling the majesty and greatness of nature tells me how great You are. The sounds I hear and the silence of the outdoors are all witnesses to You. The darkness and the light, the height and the depth, the earth and the heavens, the plants and the creatures, all came from You and exist because You have willed them. The greatness of the sky and the planets and the stars makes me feel small. The complexity of insects and flowers and earth impresses me with beauty and variety. All is from You. You control everything and give life day by day. Thank You for the life You give me each day. Thank You for placing me in this world. Thank You for letting me experience such marvelous things. Thank You for redeeming all this creation. Thank You especially for redeeming me through Your Son Jesus, who came into this world, and now brings my prayers and praise to You. **Amen.**

Lord Jesus Christ, You are the Word of God, by whom all things were made. For us and for our salvation You came down from heaven and were incarnate of the Virgin Mary. You were made man. We are now gathered before our Father in heaven in this special place. Here He seems nearer and more real than in the buildings where we are accustomed to worship. Be near us and let Your creating Spirit renew and refresh us during our time here. Let us enjoy this good creation and be responsible stewards of nature and environment. We regret that sin and evil have so corrupted and spoiled the good world that was made. Forgive us where we harm anything You have created. Help us to care for the beauty and richness of everything we experience. Let Your control over the forces of nature protect us from harm. Show us what we can do to bless the lives of others. We ask it in Your name. **Amen.**